I0559789

Conversations with Kris

Conversations with Kris

LETTERS BETWEEN A MOM AND HER MURDERED SON

Suellen M Palya

MANY**SEASONS**PRESS

Mesa, Arizona · 2023

FIRST EDITION

Conversations with Kris
Letters between a Mom and her Murdered Son

Copyright © 2023 Suellen M Palya

MANY**SEASONS**PRESS

Published by Many Seasons Press
an Imprint of Multimedia Publishing Project
123 N. Centennial Way, Suite 105
Mesa, Arizona 85201
480-939-9689 | MultimediaPublishingProject.com

Flower illustrations by Suellen M Palya

Book designed by Yolie Hernandez
(AZBookDesigner@icloud.com)

Paperback ISBN: 978-1-956203-40-0

Library of Congress Control Number: 2023948911

All rights reserved, including the right of reproduction in whole or in part in any form without permission from the publisher or author.

Printed in the United States of America.

To all families who have lost a loved one to homicide.

Contents

Foreword

IS THERE REALLY LIFE AFTER MURDER? **L**IFE AFTER YOU LEARN YOUR ADULT child was violently murdered? In these letters, one courageous parent tells you how she experiences life after the murder of her 48-year-old son.

I adopted an older Native American child, so I have some understanding of how one wonders whether their life would have been kinder had we adopted them sooner. At the same time, when our adopted child fails to graduate from high school, has an addiction problem, gets caught up in the legal system, or becomes homeless as a result of choices different from what loving parents want for their children, we might take some comfort in knowing that they are not biologically ours, and so we don't accept the blame for our child's dysfunction(s). However, they become our children the moment we bring them home.

Nevertheless, we do blame ourselves. We struggle, as Suellen Palya did, with "the would have, should have, could have, and what ifs?" Could we have done a better job? Should we have done more? What if we had acted sooner or not acted at all? We wonder if we should have given our children more money, provided shelter at the risk of losing our own sanity, and bought them more necessities at the risk of being unable to meet our own needs. We wonder time and again what to do and when to stop doing it.

I am aware of the stereotypes Native American Indians experience and the perceptions non-Natives have about American Indians. What is troubling is that so many of these stereotypes seem to be true, and yet, many of them are simply false. Working as a Clinical Psychologist for 22 years on two different Indian Reservations in Arizona provided me the opportunity to hear and bear witness to all aspects of their lives. I was a provider of information, guiding them to accept that they were more than the shame they felt because of simply who they were.

How is it possible that, even with the love of parents, our children grow into adults with dysfunctional reasoning, making poor choices and decisions that do not reflect the values they were raised with? It is a mystery that many parents examine and explore over and over again.

My 52-year-old daughter was homeless for a little more than a year. She is seriously mentally ill, untreated, unemployed, and seldom in touch. I sometimes anticipated a phone call letting me know that my daughter was dead. I never received such a phone call, but Suellen did. How does a parent get past or overcome such news from a stranger? How does a parent put their child into a grave, the very same child they once put down into a cradle or crib?

Kris, Suellen's son, may be gone, but his mother has made sure he will never be forgotten. Hers is a story about love and compassion. A story about faith and its power. Letters of love imagined being sent and received. A story about absolution.

Marilyn Stromsness, Ph.D

Preface

NO MARRIED OR SINGLE PARENTS IN MY SOCIAL CIRCLE HAD LOST A
child to homicide when my 48-year-old son, Kris, was a victim
of murder by blunt force trauma in 2017. I faced shock, loneliness,
and shame as I told friends and relatives about the event. They were
sympathetic and caring, expressing feelings of shock, sadness, and
silence as I related what the medical examiner told me.

For five years, I mentioned the tragedy with a feeling of numbness,
grieving the loss but not knowing how to mourn or express the loss of
my son. I was facilitating a GriefShare group which helped me mourn the
current loss of my husband, Paul. During one of those sessions, a woman
shared the recent loss of her husband and, several years before that, the
murder of her 21-year-old son, Stephen—finally, another mom who lost
her son to homicide.

Claudine and I shared our loss as no one else could because of
the word *murder*. She introduced me to a national group, Parents of
Murdered Children, and I attended my first national conference for survivors of loved ones lost by homicide. I heard and learned to say the word
murder without feeling shame. I became connected with a large family of
survivors who reached out and shared the name of their loved ones and
the life each one lived.

We attended workshops, memorial ceremonies, and network opportunities with one another for emotional and social support. Members of the justice system, victim advocate services, private investigators, law enforcement, healthcare, and counselors were in attendance. Workshops on trauma, coping skills, and actual therapy dogs for comfort rounded out a very impressive support system. We learned about the tragedy of cold cases, murderers not found, and incompetent justice. We signed petitions for advocates to present to parole boards in the hope of keeping a murderer off the streets and from repeating another offense.

One particular workshop inspired me to write a manuscript called *Conversations with Kris: Letters between a Mom and her Murdered Son.* The workshop is called Whispers From Heaven, and the leader encouraged participants to make a list of personal life events and the feelings they associated with each event. Participants proceeded to list events in their loved one's life and ascribe their feelings. At this point, the inspiration created a passion for me to share the following letters between Mother and Son about our life and loss journey.

It is my wish to share the love of our journey and the memories that keep Kris alive in my life. Thank you for allowing my voice to be heard with the message of healing.

Some names and events have been altered to protect the integrity of personal identification.

Letters

Dear Kris,

I am having breakfast with my husband, Paul, and our friend, Sherri, at Perkins in Minneapolis, Minnesota, when my cell phone rings; a call I will never forget. It was a female voice asking for your sister, Jan.

"Who is calling, please? My daughter is not at this number."

"You are the mom?"

"Yes, Jan is my daughter."

"This is Pam from the Medical Examiner's Office, and I am so sorry to tell you this over the phone. We found your son, Kris, deceased under the bridge of I-35 in Minneapolis this morning."

The pain in my gut made my hands shake as I gasped, "Noooooooooooo! What happened? When? Where?" My voice shakes and falters as I fight for breath to keep aware of the words I am hearing and try to comprehend in my mind the meaning of the news she has told me. How could they just call—how could they talk as if it is just—the news? I am in shock and disbelief.

"We do not have all the details yet, but we believe he died from severe blunt-force trauma. More details will be available later after the Medical Examiner has completed the autopsy. You may contact us at this number: 500-000-0000. We are so sorry for your loss. Will you be able to contact your daughter? Again, I am so sorry to bring you this news by phone."

Kris! I feel numb and speechless when the phone call ends, still not believing what I heard. You were found beaten to death? Under a local traffic overpass? How? Who? Why? It just isn't true!

Paul and Sherry guide me from the restaurant. Thoughts are causing a traffic jam in my brain as confused feelings race through the streets of my mind.

Back at the home of relatives, Paul and I discuss the message from the Medical Examiner's Office. Over time, more information arrives to piece the puzzle together, revealing the tragic event of your death. It is a comfort to know the murderer is apprehended and in custody with a million-dollar bond. He is going nowhere!

Love,
Mom

*Dear Mom

I never thought my life on earth would end because of a fight. There were many times when someone's face got too close to my space and, to defend myself, push came to shove. My height, my weight, and a good punch saved my butt most times; that, and some friends telling us to knock it off and chill. I'm sorry the news is such a shock to you and Paul. Please, tell Jan I love her. She is always there for me.

* Love ya, Kris

5

Dear Kris,

They find your naked, beaten body along an underpass of I-35 in downtown Minneapolis, Minnesota, this morning. The cause of your death is blunt force trauma, the result of your fight with Duane Blackbull at the Homeless Shelter on Dunwoody. You both sought shelter there and befriended the same woman. Duane returns to the Homeless Camp from one of his many stays in prison for domestic abuse, violence, or burglary and discovers his girl, Yolanda, spending time with you. Duane starts arguing with you, and the argument changes to blows. Your friend, Steve, sees the fight and tells me he tried to help but is held back by Duane's friends.

Later, he tells me there is a memorial gathering at the camp for you. Duane shows up and is boasting how he finished you off. That's when your friends call the authorities. Duane is arrested, held on bond, and sentenced to prison. This time it is for second-degree murder. I feel devastated that his sentence is for only seventeen and a half years; he is eligible for parole after nine years!

I attend his court sentencing, see Duane in cuffs, and read my victim's impact statement out loud before the judge, the court, and fifteen members of Duane's family and friends. His mom and sister request to appear before the judge and state, "Duane is a good boy. He got blamed for a lot of things and just took it." Hearing his mom claim her son would do no harm makes me angry, knowing his harm is your murder.

Duane asks the judge if he could turn around and speak to me. With permission, Duane looks at me and says, "I'm sorry for what I did to Kris." At that point, I gasp and sob. I feel like Jan when she stated in her victim's impact statement, "He can say he's sorry, but he's only sorry he got caught."

Love,
Mom

7

*Dear Mom,

Life in the homeless camp is survival; a roof over our heads. It is a place we help one another get through tough times with drugs and alcohol— helping one another survive—some don't. Acting out gets intense, but time to sleep it off is accepted. Winters are brutal! We are camping out huddled around a barrel fire—cardboard boxes cut the biting, freezing wind. A shelter nearby provides "three hots and a cot." Yes, the fight over Yolanda is savage. Duane and his buddies take turns with the blows while holding back my friends who want to defend me. I will spare you the gory details, as you probably read the autopsy report.

*Love, Kris

Dear Kris,

Before you were adopted at age three, we heard about the tragic events in your early years; the neglect and abandonment incidents that affect your ability to trust. In my mind and heart, I feel it was possible to provide a safe place for you to be loved, cared for, and nurtured, and you would overcome these issues. It is a real challenge. I did the best with what I knew and felt at the time. As I reflect back now, I see mistakes I made and different choices that would have been better. Please forgive me.

Love,
Mom

*Dear Mom,

Before I came to live with you, one of my earliest memories was screaming, "Get me out of here! I feel like a wolf trapped in a cage!" I am hungry; I am crying; my diaper is wet; no one hears me—I am alone in the small space of the playpen turned upside down so I cannot crawl out. Sis and Brother left, saying they were going to the store to get some food. They have no money. Sis will distract the clerk while brother hides milk and cereal in his big jacket so no one will see.

When they come home, Sis picks me up, changes my diaper, and gives me milk to drink. I rub tears from my eyes. My grubby little hands leave smudges on my face, which show the terror I feel trapped in the pen. Mom and Dad are still at the bar. Mom thinks if she drinks with Dad, they will stop drinking and go home to take care of the kids. It's a long time before they come home, and they are arguing and shouting when they come in the door. It's like this every time they come home drunk; Dad, hitting and slapping anything in his way before he goes to the couch, gets very quiet and starts to snore. Exhausted and dizzy, Mom tries to work in the kitchen, washing dishes piled in the sink, then checks to see if all the kids are asleep. Wearily, she lays on her bed, still in her clothes that smell of smoke and beer. My eyes are wide open until the quiet brings restless sleep. During the sleep, I wonder what chaos will happen next.

*Love, Kris

Dear Kris,

*T*he *beginning of your life* is filled with trouble and chaos. The beginning of my life is more calm in comparison. I am the firstborn of three children. Life is simple—Dad works in his store downtown, and Mom is home with us kids. We always have enough to eat, we have clean clothes, and we play with our friends.

I am five years old when Mom gets very sick; she is coughing red blood into her handkerchief, and the doctor says she must go to a hospital far away to rest. He calls it *tuberculosis*. Nurses stick needles in my arm and say they will come back to check my arm later. A sign is nailed to our door—QUARANTINED. I have to stay inside all the time. My friends cannot come to play, and Dad has to find someone to take care of us, clean and wash clothes, and make meals for our family. I am scared to be without Mom because she is always there to take good care of me, and I love her so much.

Love,
Mom

*Dear Mom,

Love you, too, Mom. It's easy for me to tell you that because you said it a lot when Jan and I came to live with you—not so easy to tell others, though—don't know who I can trust.

One night, my first mom and dad come home drunk again. Dad goes to the basement door, and Mom is standing there. Angrily, he rushes past her to go down the stairs. I hear screams as Mom falls down the stairs. I cry as red and blue lights flash outside the windows. Some men come in and bring my mom upstairs on a stretcher and say they were taking her to the hospital. She is not moving as they push her in front of me. She looks at me with tears in her eyes. I am afraid she will die, and then who will take care of us?

*Love, Kris

Dear Kris,

I am so sorry you remember all that trauma. Your mom didn't come back home, and someone needed to take care of you, Sis, and Brother.

When my mom went to the hospital, my dad had to find someone to take care of me, my sister, Linda, and my brother, Orbie John, who is only one year old. Dad asks Old Mrs. B if she would take care of us.

She stays with us during the day but sits moving back and forth, back and forth in a rocking chair, squawking orders to me, "Suellen! Put Linda's shoes on the correct feet—catch Orbie John before he goes out the front door. Who told you to climb up and help yourself to cookies? If you want one cookie, you must ask for one!"

Old Mrs. B didn't stay with us too long because the three of us kids were busy all the time and had a lot of energy.

Love,
Mom

*Dear Mom,

Who took care of you then if she was too old?

*Love, Kris

Dear Kris,

Dad asked *Aunt Bode,* Mom's sister, to come take care of us. I like Aunt Bode because she smiles a lot and is so pretty. One afternoon I come home from my friend's house and am so hungry. Usually, dinner is all ready, but when I open the front door, I call out, "I'm home!" and nobody answers. I call out again, "I'm home for supper," but no one answers. The shadows of the day lay in long ribbons across the floor, no lights are on, and no one is in the kitchen. I feel all alone, sit in a chair and cry big sobs. "Where is everybody? Where is anybody?" I walk to the telephone and call Dad at work.

"Daddy! I just got home for supper, and no one is here."

"Where is Aunt Bode?"

"She's not here," I sob into the phone. Now I really feel all alone and so scared as big tears drip from my eyes.

"Don't cry, Susie!" Daddy says, "I'll come home right away."

I am still crying when Daddy walks in the back kitchen door, gives me a big hug, and says, "It's okay, now, I'm here with you."

Just then, the back door opens, and Aunt Bode walks in, holding Linda's hand. Her daughter, Cleone, is carrying Orbie John.

"Why weren't you home to fix supper?" Dad asks Aunt Bode.

"Oh! We got to visit with friends, and it got later and later; you know how that goes!" she stated with a smile on her face.

"Well, Susie called me at work, crying that she is all alone and no one is here to make supper. I pay you to be here at home with all the kids and have supper ready, and if you can't do that—you will have to leave."

"Okay! I will!" Aunt Bode spat back. "And you're on your own for supper." She spins around on her new red high heels; her skirt swirls behind her as she grabs Cleone's hand and marches out the back door.

We had scrambled eggs and toast for supper that night, and when Daddy tucks us into bed, I ask, "Who will take care of us now?"

"Don't you worry about that, Susie! I'll find someone."

That is when Mabel came to stay with us.

Love,
Mom

*Dear Mom,

I remember the night my mom left with all the red and blue lights flashing! After they take Mom away on the stretcher, a stranger lifts me gently out of the pen. My eyes dart around, looking for Sis and Brother. Where did they go? It is dark and cold outside, and I call out for Sis. She doesn't answer!

The stranger says, "Sis is coming with us to Carrie's house. You will all stay there. You're going to be okay."

I didn't feel okay. I am cold, and my diapers are wet. My eyes dart back and forth, watching for danger. What could happen next? The stranger wraps a warm blanket around me and holds me in her lap as we get into a car. I start to scream like a wolf again like I am back in a cage. Big, big tears are rolling down my cheeks. I don't like being locked up!! Another stranger comes toward the car holding the hand of a little girl. It is Sis! The car door opens, and Sis sits next to me. My screams become sobs. Sis looks at me with big brown eyes, and I can see she is scared, too. I feel a little safer as Sis puts her hand on my arm. Still feeling trapped, I look out the car window and see Brother get into another car.

My eyes dart from Sis to Brother, and I feel so scared that my whole body is shaking. Brother is leaving us and going away. I want to say goodbye to him, hold him close, and not let go of him.

*Love, Kris

Dear Kris,

I know you have the best care you could have when a foster family provides you with a safe home, good food to eat, and the attention you need to feel accepted and secure. Your mom did not come home again, and you did not see your father. He tried to find relatives to take care of his children, but there was no home safe enough. A foster home was a safe place for you to stay until you could find a "forever home." Mabel gave me and my brother and sister the care we needed while Mom was gone for one and a half years. You had lots of foster brothers and sisters who cared for you.

Love,
Mom

*Dear Mom,

It is fun at the foster home. Kids play with me, I get new clothes, and the food was not too bad. My eyes still dart here and there—looking for Mom—Dad—Sis—Brother. Where did they go? Will they come back?

There are lots of toys to play with—I sit on top of a yellow and black train on tracks that go round and round on the carpet. It's fun to climb up and down and ride around. I climb on all the furniture, too, still looking for danger. Will Sis come back?

*Love, Kris

Dear Kris,

I wonder if my mom will come back, too. I feel very scared of Mabel. She has a small, round, black box over one of her eyes. I hide behind my dad, not because I was shy or because she is someone I don't know.

Mabel is a family friend who was at picnics on the farm where my dad grew up. This is the first time I had seen her up close and heard her talk.

"Come here, Suellen, and let me see how big you are. Your daddy told me about his three cute children. Here! I'll move over to make room so you can sit next to me."

Slowly and cautiously, I move closer to Mabel, with a little nudging from Dad, and soon find myself sitting next to her up close. She has a fresh smell of soap about her as she reaches out her thin, sun-tanned hand to gently touch my arm.

I am curious and ask, "Why do you cover your eye with that black box?"

Mabel answers as a matter-of-fact, "I hurt my eye."

It becomes easy to be around her with my curiosity satisfied. I feel the warmth and comfort of her friendship. It

doesn't take long to see a beautiful person I can trust. I don't notice the round black box anymore. It didn't scare me or seem odd.

Love,
Mom

*Dear Mom,

I am three years old when you come to visit me at my foster home.
I am riding on the black and yellow train, round and round, round and
round as you smile and talk with me. I remember jumping off the train,
running around the room, jumping on the couch, and crawling along the
back of the couch where you sit. You seem nice, but I am scared; more new
people around. Where is Sis? Where is Brother? Later, Sis comes back with
you, and we ride in your big blue car to King Leo's, a hamburger place with
a playground. I like the French fries and hamburger, but most of all, I am
with Sis again. With Sis around, it feels like getting a gift for Christmas. It
is the best gift I could hope to get—my family. I ask, "Can we all go home
together?"

You tell me, "Not today, but soon."

*Love, Kris

Dear Kris,

I want my family to be all together, too. My mom comes back home from the hospital. Mabel stays to help her make meals, do housework, and watch us kids. Mom needs a lot of rest, but each day she becomes stronger. She would color with me in my big coloring book and help me cut out paper dolls. Mom lived twenty-three more years. You meet her when we adopt you and Sis and bring you to your "forever home." Our family is bigger now—a mom, a dad, a little brother, you, and Sis. It is two weeks before Christmas, and you two children are the gifts added to our family. There are new clothes to buy, shoes, and boots. The store clerk asks me what size you wear and looks at me with a strange expression when I tell her, "I don't know because I have never bought shoes for my children before today." I explain we just adopted you and brought you to our home to stay.

My family loves you. It doesn't take us long to become a big family with lots of relatives who get together for Christmas dinner, go to church, and spend time getting to know one another.

Love,
Mom

*Dear Mom,

It's a big house! There is a fireplace and lots of toys and room to play. I sleep in a room with a new little brother you adopted before Sis and I came. Little brother sleeps in a crib... I'm a big brother now! One night I had a bloody nose and wiped the blood on the wall with my fingers. You came to clean me up and then cleaned the wall, too. You are taking care of me—I don't talk much, but I feel safe because there is no cage around me. It's quiet when something goes wrong, and you speak calmly about fixing and making things better. You help me stop my bloody nose, and I begin to feel brave. I feel good again and think about sliding down the snowy hill on our sleds tomorrow.

*Love, Kris

Dear Kris,

*W*e adopted three kids—ages one-and-a-half to five years old. It is very busy in our household—eating three meals a day together at the big table is important; keeping a schedule and following a routine brings stability to all five of us. You, little brother, and Sis play well together—you all like Star Wars—Sis is Princess Leia, little brother is Luke Skywalker, and you are Darth Vader. We all color together or cut and paste Valentines, frost Holiday cookies and make shapes with clay. When we color hard-boiled eggs for Easter, your favorite thing to do is drink the colored vinegar water. I read storybooks to all of you, and we watch Captain Kangaroo and Mr. Rogers on television. A big family is fun!!!

Love,
Mom

*Dear Mom,

Those are some good times. I remember when Dad showed us how to use hammers and pound nails into a piece of board. I make a box to hide in, and little brother builds a wooden pinball machine. We play in the hills behind our house and take sandwiches for a picnic. It is fun to explore, and we know where all the trails are. Remember when we built a fire by the river and roasted hot dogs and roasted marshmallows for S'mores? They are a favorite of mine 'cause they get gooey and burnt from the hot fire.

*Love, Kris

Dear Kris,

S'*mores with gooey*, brown marshmallows are a favorite of mine, too. When it is time for you to go to school, there is trouble at the bus stop. Kids call names and push you around. Sis is with you, and it is hard for her, too. Kids are using the N-word because your skin color is darker than theirs. It hurts your feelings, and you feel different and sad when they call you names. One day, you just sit outside the school instead of going inside. The teacher called me and asked if you were home ill. I drive to school, and there you are, sitting outside all by yourself. I tell you that you don't have to like it, but you do have to go to school.

Love,
Mom

*Dear Mom,

Kids are mean—they say I am a bad kid—something about Indians and Cowboys. Teacher is nice, but kids are mean. Sis is my friend, and I feel safe with her. I try to read—my eyes don't work. Schoolwork is hard. I don't like school.

*Love, Kris

28

Dear Kris,

*G*lasses help you see better, and you learn better, too. It seems hard for you to concentrate or ask questions. Captain Kangaroo, Sesame Street, and Mr. Rogers held your attention, and soon you learned the alphabet. You especially like to sing each song you hear.

Love,
Mom

*Dear Mom,

I never did like to read like Sis did. Watching TV is a good way for me to learn because the songs, colors, and movement hold my attention. Playing games on a board is fun, too. Best of all, I like big dump trucks. Oh! Learning to ride a bike is awesome—I go really fast! "Speedy" is my middle name!

*Love, Kris

Dear Kris,

Yes! You are the kid who gets your knees scraped up or falls out of bed and needs seven stitches on your chin. Consequences don't concern you—it is full-speed ahead—and you don't seem to mind—you rarely cry, so strong is your armor of protection, so high your threshold of pain. I am not sure I could handle all your challenges. I wonder if I am a good-enough mom? I feel concerned about helping you feel strong and make good choices before something becomes dangerous and hurtful. I am not sure how to help you think about safety. I want to protect you from harm, and I want you to learn how to help yourself.

Love,
Mom

*Dear Mom,

What happened? We leave the nice big house and move to a small apartment in a huge building with lots of big students at a university. We are still a family, but something is not right. Dad is gone a lot or always reading and too busy to spend time with us. You are quiet and grumpy. You still do fun things with us, like making snowmen outside our apartment window. We all go to the playground nearby and make new friends with kids who can't see us because they are blind. All of us still have fun anyway.

One summer, little brother and friend Darrin go down to the creek. In the water on the rocks are crayfish. We have fun when we find them under the rocks and try to catch them before they scurry away.

Darrin said, "Come here, you little bastard!"

I ask him, "Did you catch a crayfish?"

Little brother answers, "No! It's a bastard!"

I remember making gingerbread men with cookie dough. I draw a picture on paper, cut it out, and trace it on the flat cookie dough. It bakes in the oven, and when it is cool, I decorate it with frosting. The gingerbread men disappear but surprise us on Christmas morning.

Little brother and I try to make a chocolate cake with flour, milk, and chocolate chips. It flashes brightly when we put the tin pan in the microwave oven. The microwave didn't work for a few days!

Aunt Lori comes to take care of us when you go to a hospital. Will you come back?

*Love, Kris

Dear Kris,

I'm sorry I am grumpy. I feel depressed leaving the nice, big home and moving into a small apartment. I do not feel needed and feel alone most of the time. Your dad and I grow away from each other and do not talk about it. It bothers me a lot when I need an operation that takes away my ability to birth any children. I love all of you, and adoption was not the problem. I have to learn to like who I am as a woman. This is a struggle for me at this time, and, unfortunately, we all have a hard time with my anger and depression. I am doing the best I can at the time. Please forgive me.

Love,
Mom

*Dear Mom,

You sit with us—read books—watch TV—make things. I'm sorry you are sad. Is that why you and Dad got a divorce? Us kids think it is our fault that we aren't behaving; we don't know. Why do we move with Dad and take the dog with us, and Sis gets to stay with you? Now, another woman who has two kids moves in with us. Little brother and I travel on the bus to come and see you. It's hard to say goodbye when we leave you at the bus station. See you at Christmas.

Love, Kris

Dear Kris,

Oh! *Those years apart* from you and little brother are very hard times. Sometimes I drive down to see you, stay in a motel, and watch TV together. We drive to visit Sis in Job Corps, and on the way home, we stop at Pizza Hut. There are just a few people there. When you, little brother, and I walk in, I hear a man tell a little kid who is standing up in the booth, "Sit down, or I'll sic that Indian on you."

We sit to order our pizza, eat our meal, and when it is time to leave, I tell you, "Boys, go to the car and wait for me."

I walk over to the booth and tell the man, "You know, saying to your child that he should sit down or you will sic that Indian on him makes it very hard to get along in this world."

The man replies, "I didn't say it," pointing a finger at his friend, "he did."

At that moment, I say, "I don't care who it was, it just makes it difficult for people to get along." Having said that, I turn around and walk away. I am shaking as I turn and walk away. It takes a lot of courage and strength the first time I take a vocal stand to stop oppression, Kris. I am aware you face oppression and prejudice a lot, and we need to speak out against this injustice.

Love, Mom

*Dear Mom,

I wonder what you say to those guys—proud of you for standing up for us—I feel I can count on you to have my back. I'm sorry for the times I take advantage of you—stealing your jewelry to sell for cash—asking you for a few bucks to fix something on my car and using it for weed and whiskey. That way of life seems familiar to me—it makes the world less hateful. After I leave Job Corps in Montana, I travel or hitchhike from one place to another. I find people like me who only want a place to eat, sleep and drink. We stand on street corners asking for handouts hoping for a buck or two for a cheap drink. Life is easy, sleeping from one drink to another. Shelters provide a warm meal and a cot when the weather is bad. Other times, a homeless camp has space to stretch out and hang together with others who like the easy life.

*Love, Kris

Dear Kris,

I worried when I would not hear from you during the ten years you went AWOL from Job Corps in Montana. Was it less hateful living in the homeless camps? I waited and waited to hear from you; I had no idea where you were or how you were getting along. I attended Al-Anon and Nar-Anon meetings and learned about the family disease of alcoholism and drug addiction. You spent time in Juvenile Detention for absenting from home, substance abuse, and behavior issues. Al-Anon taught me the only reason for membership is having a friend or family member with an alcohol problem. It was a program for me to examine my own powerlessness over alcohol that gave me guidance and courage to change the things I can, accept the things I could not change, and learn the wisdom to know the difference. It is comforting to know I did not cause the problem, and I could not cure it. When I feel I cannot trust what you say or do, I wait for you to give me reasons to trust you.

After ten years, you come back to the Midwest from California. You tell me of your experiences with the Bloods and Cripps gangs in California. You ended up leaving California and were apprehended for unauthorized use of a motor vehicle. You are jailed, released in Colorado as a State's witness, and told never to return. You work your way back to North Dakota, reunite with family, and tell them of your excursions. There are stories about using hallucinatory

37

drugs, seeing elephants climb walls and hang from the ceiling, and about you sleeping under the Golden Gate Bridge and finding a local shelter for three hots and a cot.

There is another tale you mention about your job riding the range along the southern border of the United States. The rancher hired you to ride a horse around a large area to patrol the border between the United States and Mexico. It was a lonely job, but you say you enjoyed being alone out on the prairie under the stars at night. You are a great storyteller as I listen to the lilt of your voice.

It is great having you stay with me for a week. You install a screen door in the garage for better air circulation in the condo where I live. It feels good to have someone to share meals with again, as I recently lost my second husband, Roy, to stomach cancer, and I am grieving being left alone. It is lonely living in a condo by myself. Making meals for one isn't easy, and life is empty as time passes slowly. You stay only a short time and are gone, "who knows where?"

Love,
Mom

*Dear Mom,

Staying in one place for a long time is not my style. The adventure of moving on is addicting for me.

*Love, Kris

Dear Kris,

*Y*ou are a talented man experiencing risky behavior and surviving to tell about it. You are a bright young man who is street-smart with a big heart. I have no idea how long you will live this way, and during your absence, my only comfort each day is that the Red Cross has not called to tell me you are deceased. I continue to ask God to watch over your safety and guide you. Meanwhile, I commit myself to live each day to its fullest and take care to be there when you contact me again.

It is during this time that I meet Paul. I am retired from my job as an Academic Counselor at the University of North Dakota and working at a local Hallmark Store. The lady I work with knows I am widowed and told me her neighbor, who is recently widowed, wants to go for coffee and visit with a woman. She asks me if she may give him my phone number.

I say, "Sure! I like coffee."

Well, the guy never called, and a year later, she asks again. Thinking this guy will never call, I agree. She makes him call twenty minutes later, and Paul and I agree to meet for coffee at the Northside's Perkins. I tell your Sis that I am meeting this guy on a blind date for coffee the next morning.

"Noooooo!" she said. "Mom, you've been hurt too many times, and I don't want you to be hurt again."

"I'll drive my own car, and if it doesn't go well, I'll excuse myself and leave."

Paul walks into Perkins with a cane, hunched over because, as I learned from our conversation, he contracted polio when he was nine. As we visit, I see a good man with a sense of humor. We laugh together for an hour and a half; we decide to meet again for coffee.

Well, our coffee dates lead to lunch dates, and eventually, he asks if I will meet him at the Bronze Boot, a local dinner club. He asks me if I would mind driving my own car, and I agree. Well, I walk in, and Paul is seated at the head of a table for six, and two other couples drop open their mouths when I walk in. They had asked Paul who would fill the empty chair, and Paul had arranged for me to meet his neighbors! A year later, he asked me to visit him in Mesa, Arizona, for a couple of weeks. He winters there as the ice and snow are a physical challenge for him.

That was the beginning of our committed relationship for almost fifteen years before he died.

Love,
Mom

*Dear Mom,

Paul is a good man, and I am happy for you. We meet together in Minneapolis when you come to visit his grown kids in Minnetonka and St Paul. My friend and I make our way across town in the truck I am given to drive to my job as a computer operator, designing machine parts. Lunch by your motel was the best meal I ever had. Thanks for buying the tank of fuel to get back.

*Love, Kris

Dear Kris,

Thanks for friending me on Facebook with your Wolf identity. It means a lot to me to connect with you again and for you to meet Paul. Now he knows all my family. You have seven years of sobriety at this time. You tell me about a day you were waiting in a line in downtown St Paul, and a group of Natives walked up to you and asked why you were waiting in line.

You told them, "I'm waiting for my crack cocaine!"

They say, "You don't need to be here. Come with us! We have a warm meal and a way for you to stay out of this line. You can receive outpatient treatment, have a job, and a truck for transportation."

It is at this time that we meet again in person. My heart was overjoyed to have contact with you again. I so miss you each time we are distanced from one another. You will always be my son; I will always be your mother. I thank God again for watching over you.

Love,
Mom

*Dear Mom,

Those people who found me on the streets are good people. They keep their promises to care for me until I can be on my own again. Going through outpatient treatment one more time helps me get a grip on my addiction enough to stay sober for the time it took to get that computer job on the graveyard shift. Working at night fits my schedule as a night owl. You are always there for me, Mom. It must be hard for you to see me, and then I take off again without a word. Paul is a good guy, and I'm glad to see you happy. Oh! Thanks for the fuel and lunch.

*Love, Kris

Dear Kris,

*W*hen we say goodbye and I wish you safe travels, I wonder when the next time will be, and if we will meet again. Each time we drive to Minneapolis, I think of you and wonder where you are. I look closely at the homeless on street corners asking for handouts, hoping I might find you again. I hesitate to give money handouts to support unhealthy drug or alcohol habits. It is hard to understand those who have dogs with them and are smoking cigarettes, a very expensive habit. Kris, I would not choose that way of life for myself, but I accept it is a style of life that challenges the daring, risk-taking person you are. I pray every day God will keep you in His loving care.

I expect the Red Cross will contact me when and if your life is in danger, and yet the day the medical examiner tells me they found your naked, deceased body, the finality is a shock. Your life on the streets has come to a tragic end. No longer will you be asking for money to repair a flat tire when I know you don't own a vehicle or live through the cold winter weather or the hot seething summers on the streets.

Gone are the phone calls when you ask for money to reach the end of the month. Gone are the visits where you have no place to stay, and I pay for a night in a local, cheap motel so you can have a roof over your head. Gone are the trips to the grocery store to pay for the food you need rather than give you cash. I want to help, but I have learned through tough love that some help would just enable you to be irresponsible in situations where you should be able to help yourself and not depend on me to do it for you.

Love,
Mom

*Dear Mom,

Yes! You got smart, and I realize I am on my own. You know I can figure problems out for myself—I just need to be sober long enough to take that responsibility. I tell you over the phone that I have quit drinking when I am actually sitting in the bar with friends buying a round of drinks on payday.

*Love, Kris

Dear Kris,

Yes! That is the last earthly contact we have. I drive to Fry's grocery store in Mesa and am pushing the grocery cart into Produce when my cellphone rings with your name on the display. I answer and hear only people talking and laughing. I try to get your attention.

"Kris! Kris!" I shout into the phone. After a few minutes, you take your phone out of your pocket and answer me.

"Mom! Did I call you? My phone never rang,"

"Yes! You must have butt dialed me."

"Well, how are you, Mom?"

"I'm fine. Where are you?"

"I'm in the bar with friends, and I'm buying a round 'cause it's payday."

"Well, Kris! We can visit another time."

"Ok, Mom! Bye! Love you!"

"Love you, too, Kris!"

So ended our last earthly conversation! Two months later, the medical examiner calls to say you were murdered!

Love, Mom

*Dear Mom,

It is a good thing we said, "goodbye and love you."

*Love, Kris

Dear Kris,

It is now six years since the news of your murder tears loose threads I cling to on the frayed tapestry of your life on earth. My fear has been confirmed by your early passing at 48 years old. I never imagined the day or time I would receive the news of your early demise, but I anticipated it, nonetheless.

My family gathers around that time to celebrate the Schultz Family Farm's Centennial. Many of us gather on the farm near Donnybrook, North Dakota. Most family members show care and concern as we talk about the events related to your murder, and they, in turn, speak of the memories they have of you as a treasured, valuable member of our large relationship. None can relate to my grief as a mom who just lost one of her children and the horrible shock and pain I am carrying with the news of your tragic murder at the hands of another so far away in the Cities.

As time moves on, other family and close friends lend an ear to hear details of your murder, yet remain mute and unable to comprehend the pain this mother carries after the tragic loss of her son. I have been in shock for quite a time, able to feel the grief yet unable to express the mourning. Tragedies like a murder are incomprehensible. Normal grief for losing loved ones is usually the result of old age or disease. No one in my social circle has experienced a loss of a loved one to homicide.

Until one day, I serve as a facilitator for a grief group of those who have lost loved ones. A young woman stands up to relate she recently lost her husband and had previously lost her son when he was murdered at a party.

Now, Kris! This was not a coincidence. I believe God is reaching out to me with a message that this person is there to guide me through mourning my loss of you. You know I am a trained grief counselor who can guide other people through the grief process. I attended GriefShare through our church when Paul died two years before, and the leader asked me to stay on to serve as a facilitator. Through this group, I find the opportunity to find and share with others who have similar losses. Claudine drove me to Scottsdale one weekend for the National Conference of Parents of Murdered Children.

Love,
Mom

*Dear Mom,

You shared your Christian values with Sis and me on our baptism and attending Sunday School and Church every Sunday. I remember being Confirmed. The teachings of the Great Spirit in my Native culture and the ways of the Shaman returned as part of my nature when I became acquainted with many Native friends. Values of Native culture were shared with me at the Mandan Reform School. You visited and met the Sioux Elder who was helping me learn how to tan a buffalo hide. My involvement with the Native American Indian Movement in the Cities shared history and Native beliefs. I realize that our voices need to be heard. My participation in demonstrations strengthened my bond with my Indian culture by meeting Russell Means and other influential leaders.

*Love, Kris

Dear Kris,

*Y*ou sought out opportunities to learn about your culture—something I could only encourage you to do as the values and beliefs of the white German, French, and Irish cultures were a part of my upbringing.

Love,
Mom

Dear Mom,

I remember going to Pow Wows at the University of North Dakota when we lived on campus. We had lessons about the Round Dance. You tried to dress us in traditional Indian dress for one Halloween and found out from a Native person what a stereotype it was. The Father of the Native family will have a ceremonial dance dress made for the daughter and a ceremonial outfit for the sons. We did go to a lot of picnics on campus and saw many people of color. My birth mom was Metis Chippewa, and my birth dad was Canadian Chippewah from the Rolling River Band in Canada, so by birth, Sis and I had dual citizenship. You adopted us six years before the Indian Child Welfare Act was passed by Congress in 1978. It stated Native children are no longer placed in non-Native homes.

Well, anyway, it worked out. We grew to live together despite our hardships and still love and respect one another, don't you know?

*Love, Kris.

September 23, 2022

Dear Kris,

Yes, my son. Love and respect is what it's all about. We remained close until the end of your earthly life, and I continue to honor your memory, remembering your life here on earth and the way you chose to live it--and you lived it just the way you wanted.

Today, I am sitting in the recliner sewing by hand a red and black ribbon together. When a pin is sewn on the back, it is worn by members of Parents of Murdered Children (POMC) to honor our loved ones lost by acts of violence. I wear my ribbon with reverence to your memory and the life we share together forever.

Love, Your Mom

*Dear Mom,

I feel honored as you keep me alive in your memory and share my life story with others.

Love,
Your son Kris

Dear Kris,

Today is National Day of Remembrance for all loved ones whose life on earth ended in tragic, violent deaths to homicide. Survivors gathered at a picnic in Granada Park near Phoenix, Arizona. Similar events are held all over the United States. A guest table is prepared for our honored guests, and your mom decorates it with a picnic basket and four place settings on a red and white checkered tablecloth. Each survivor takes a small wooden heart and a marker and writes the name of their loved one and a message. I write, "Love ya, Kris. Mom." The hearts are placed on the table near the Memory Wall, where pictures of loved ones are posted. You are holding your dog in the picture.

All the survivors gather around and share their stories. It helps to talk about the tragic event that ended your journey on earth.

Guess what! Your mom is asked to help release white doves from their cage at a certain time in the ceremony. During the music, I raise the crate's door to release the doves. What a powerful whoosh of feathers as the doves head back to their home in Gilbert, several miles away.

The beautiful sight of doves in flight over the lake releases emotions I hadn't been able to express; I opened my mouth and began to sob as I raised my arm to heaven. Immediately, I am hugged by friends Kim and Marie. They knew I needed that comfort for the loss of my 48-year-old child, named Kris.

My soul grieves to have lost you, but the 48 years we journeyed together is a gift, and you are now at peace after finally coming home. Your cremains are laid to rest in the cemetery plot where my second husband, Roy, is buried in Tabor, Minnesota. When he died, you brought an Eagle feather for his heavenly journey. Kris! You are forever in my heart, holding your precious memory.

Love,
Mom

Left to right: Kris and his little
brother on their Hot Wheels. Uncle
Orv and the children. The three
siblings when they were young.

Mabel and her two grave markers.

THE LAST CALL (June 2017)

You lived the life of a homeless wanderer

Seeing the world as you chose.

Each day, my assurance was,

"The Red Cross has not called"

To tell me you were gone.

Staying healthy was my goal, to be able to tell you,
"I love you, Kris" when you would call, text

Or Friend me on Facebook.

Prayers, music, and photos kept you in my heart each day.

During your seven years sobriety we met in Minneapolis for lunch,

Not realizing that would be the last time we would see each other.

The last time we talked was your butt call from the bar during
my weekly visit to the grocery store 500 miles away.

You heard me calling your name from your
pocket and asked if you had called me?

You told me you had just gotten paid and
were treating some friends to drinks.

That was your last call; the memory of your
voice still lingers in my mind.

Fearing a call from the Red Cross finally arrived
from the Medical Examiner's office.

They found your deceased, naked
body by the interstate in
downtown Minneapolis.

You are now home with
us for eternal rest,

The Last Call.

> *I love you, my son!*
> *Love, Mom*

Dear mom,

High. How are you? Me, doin pretty good. Just thought I'd drop you a line or two, Don't have much to say. I'm just sittin here listening to Guns-n-Roses and waiting for San to come home from work. Krystal's sitting here being as wierd as she can possibly be. But I love her all the same. I take care of Krystal during the evening, till San comes home, to pay my rent. It's alright but I wish I could find a job. I got hired for the ag-expo. I'm gonna be a cook in a consession stand on the fair grounds. But it's only for a few dayz. But it's noter extra cash on hand to buy some new clothes. More than likely I'll buy a pair of boots 'cause I'm sick of these darn shoes. They bug the hell out of my legs and makes them sore. And they're uncomfy on my feet.

Thank you for the christmas gifts. I appreciate all you did to try and make me feel comfortable but I wuz still having troubles adjusting. It's gonna take me time to be able to be free in my little castle I have built around my heart. But it's is coming down bit by slow bit. I'm gonna, and gotta, rehabilitate myself from everything that's happened and that is happening. Like my divorce and a few other things. It's hard but San and my friends are helpful in that aspect. They keep me so busy sometimes I don't know whether I'm coming, going, where I been, and where I'm going. It's not a helpless feeling. It's just that I get so involved in the activities, ▬ that it's all that's on my mind. But like most everything else it has to come to an end and then I get to be bored and that's when I start thinking and it's hard to overcome all the guilty and angry feelings I have. And the sadness and sometimes emptiness or

---

This letter was written by Kris and it was found in 2022 by his mom, Suellen. It was in the Christmas card address book. Page one of two, page two is on the following page along with Kris' tombstone.

Lonely feelings occur in there too. I still wake-up every morning at 2:00 am sharp from a living nightmare. And what I mean by that is it's something that happened to me a couple years ago. That plus Tammy are still in my dream department. But I try not to dwell on them too much. I try to stay as busy as possible. Plus is I do get down I've always got my friends to turn to. So everything works out quite well for me. Right now I'm making pork chops for Krystal and I. Gad! This child can go non-stop all day and it's a heck of a job trying to keep up with her. We got her a "Kitty", as Krystal calls it. Dan calls it "Meusky". I just call it Bonehead like the lady we got her from did. It's a nice cat though.

Well, I got another letter I got to write so I got to sign off for now.

Take care and God Bless

Love,
Kris

FOREVER IN OUR HEARTS
KRISTIE JAMES
STEINKE
AUG. 27, 1968 — JUNE 9, 2017

www.ingramcontent.com/pod-product-compliance
Lightning Source LLC
Chambersburg PA
CBHW051237120626
46547CB00013B/1689